We Like

BASTARD

Brilliant Swear Word To Color

For Stress Releasing

Bear Smithbet

Happy Coloring!

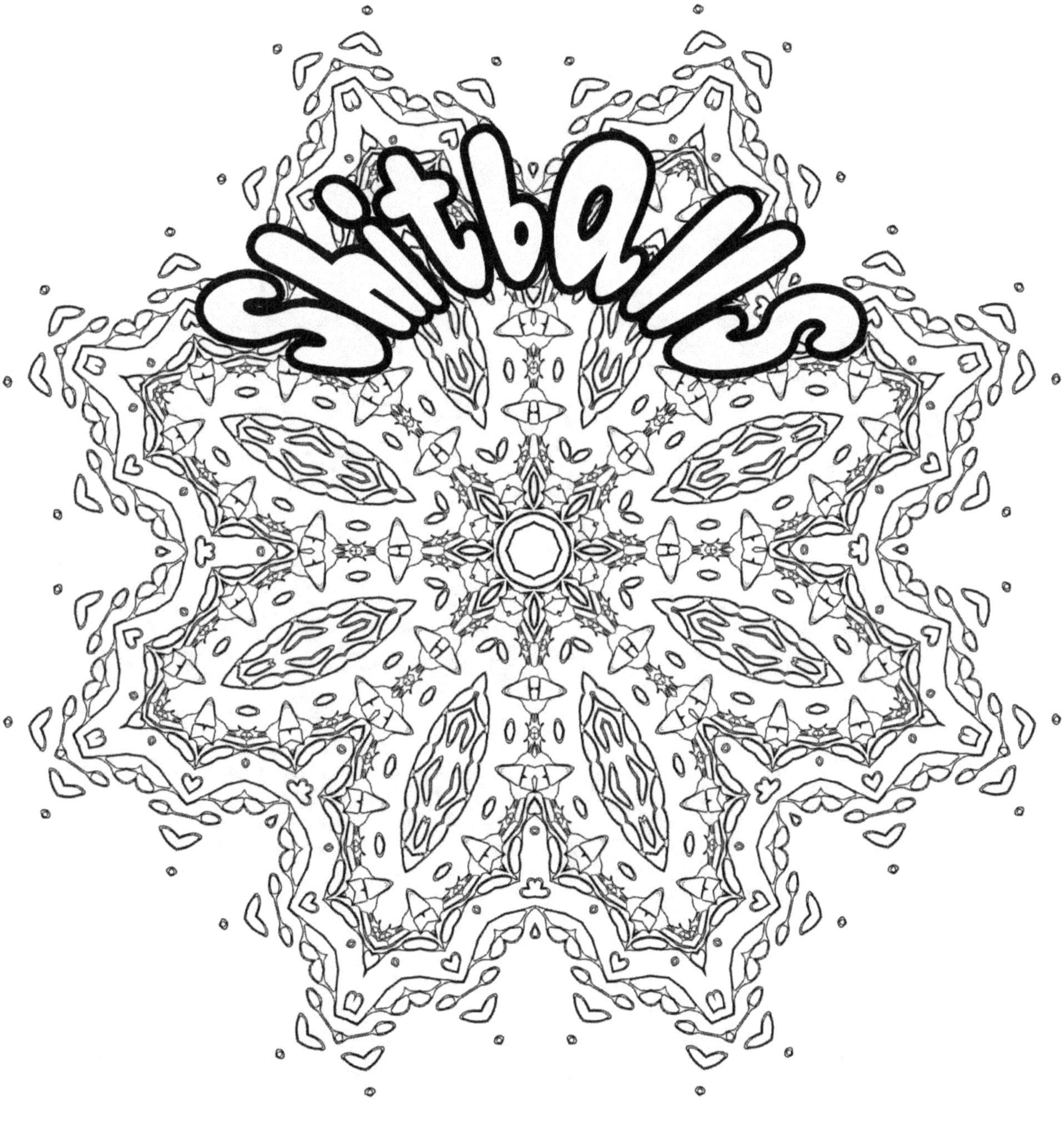
shitballs

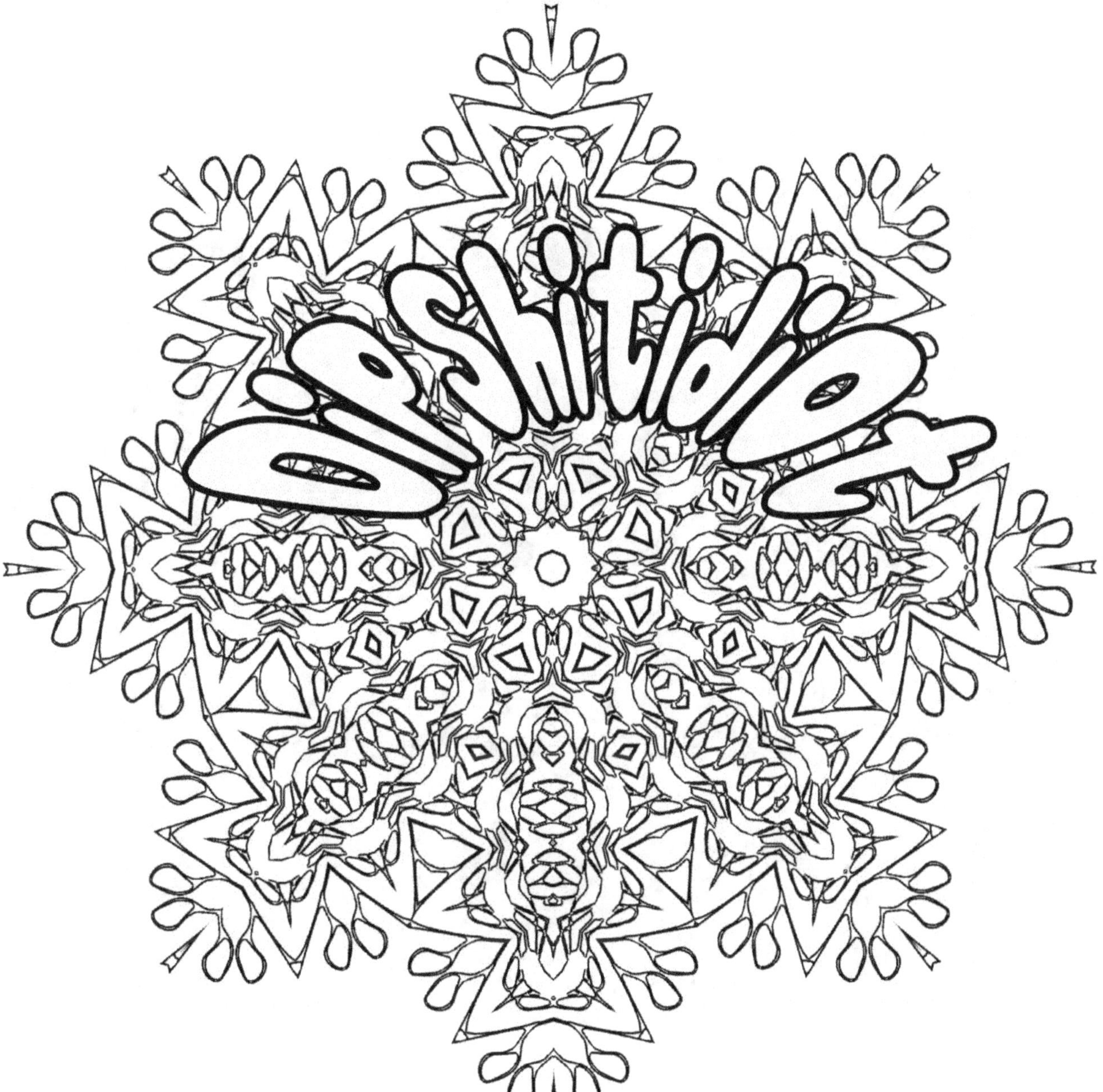
dipShitidiot

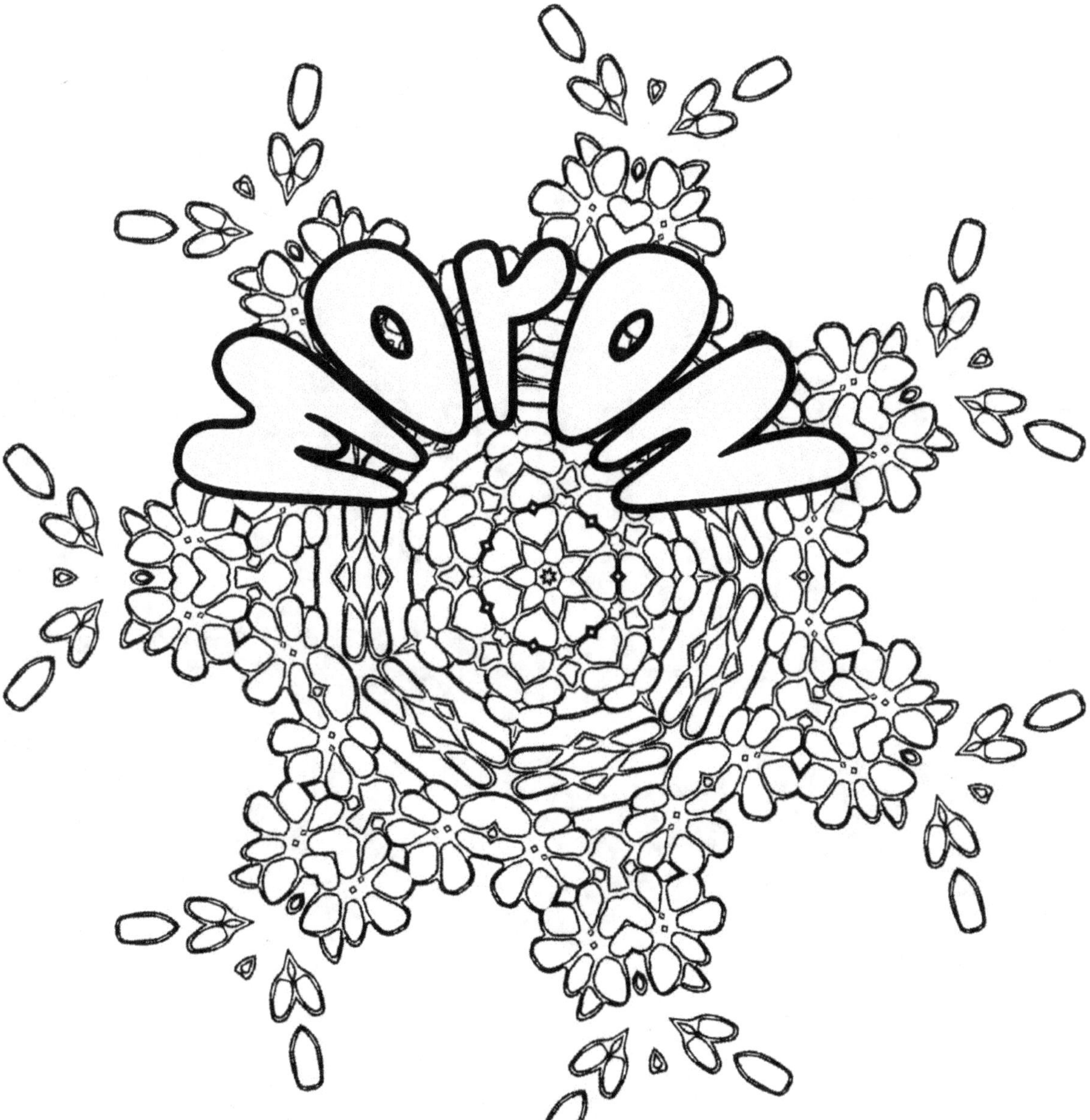
MORON

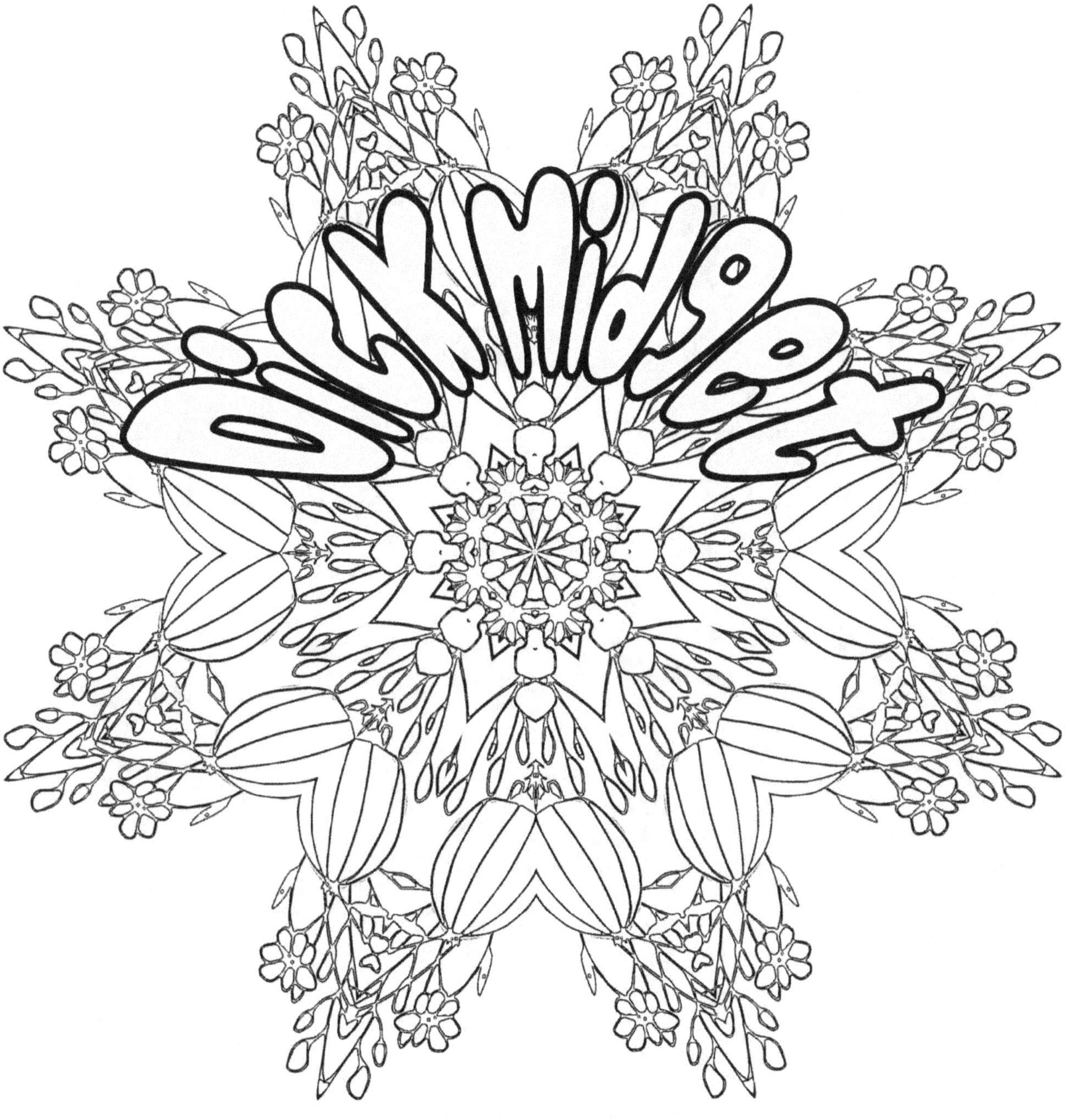
Dick Midget

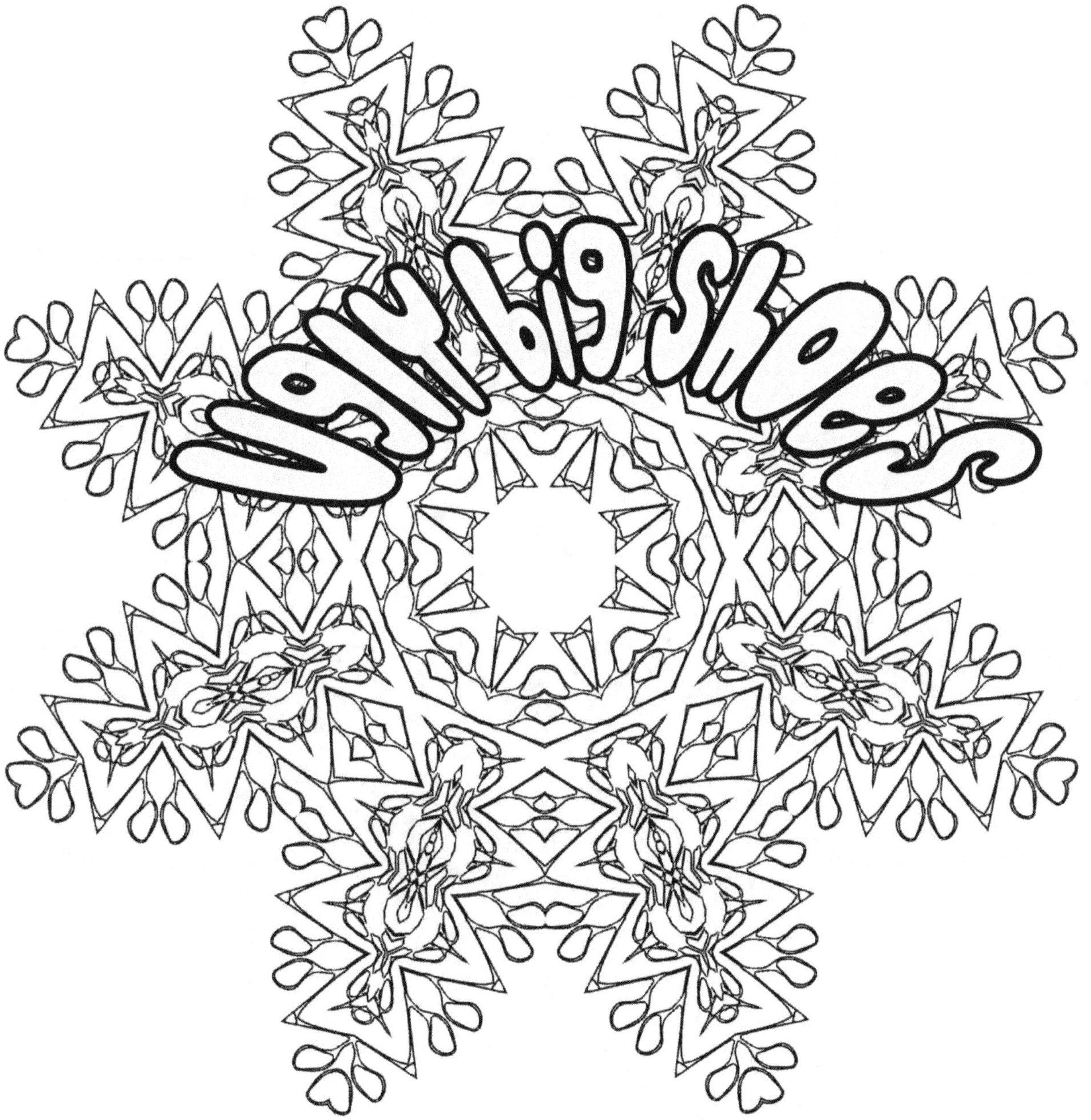
very big shoes

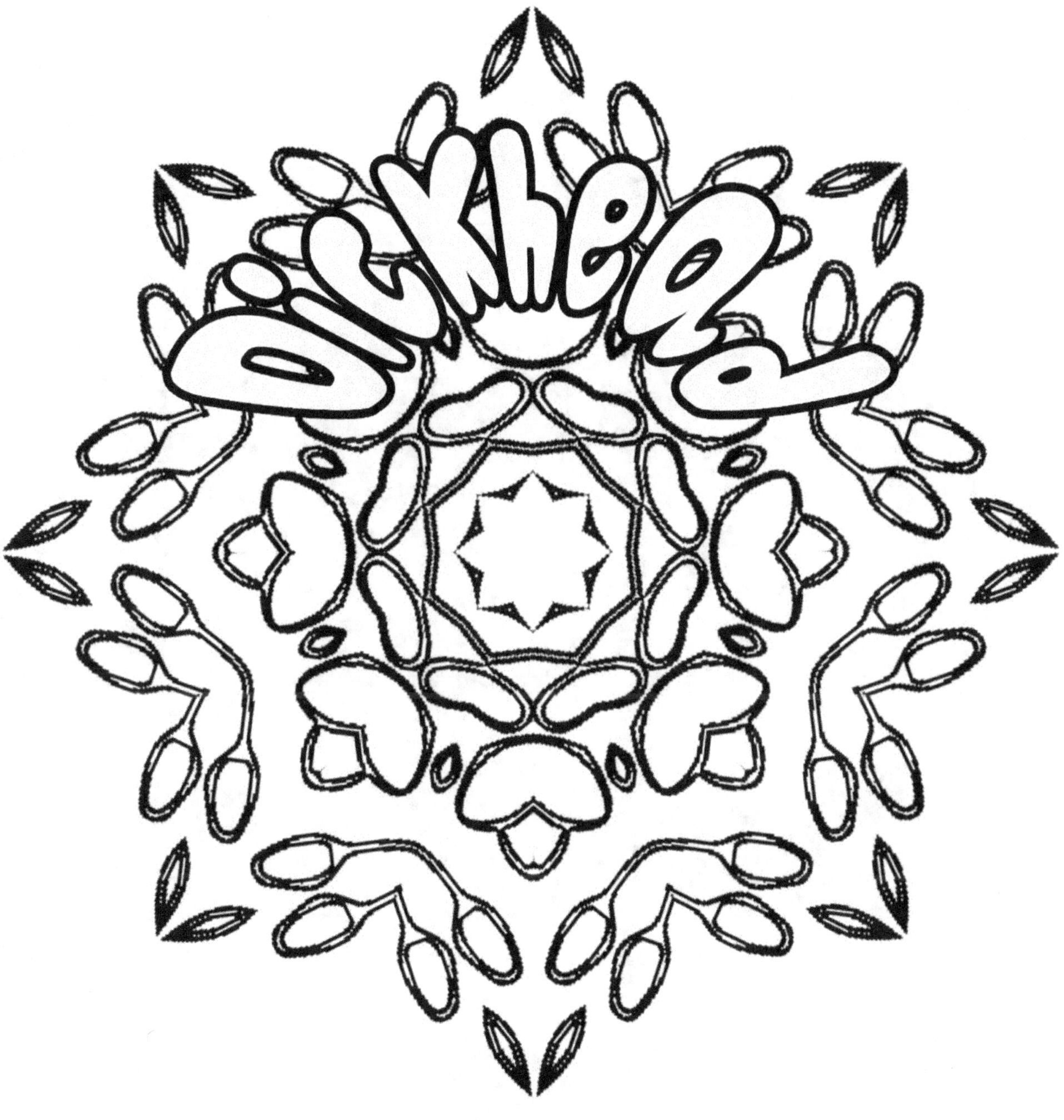
Dickhead

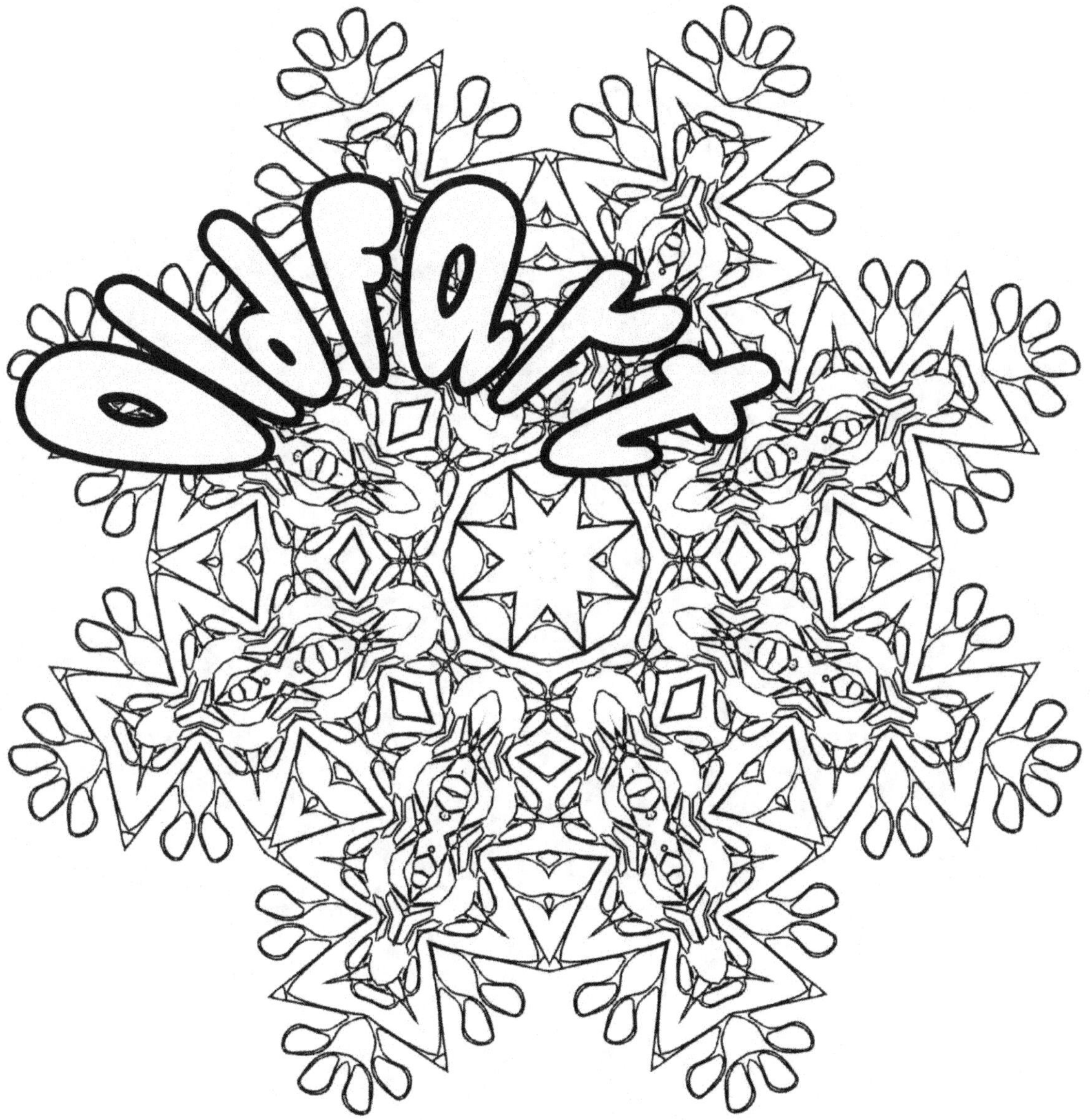
Old Fart

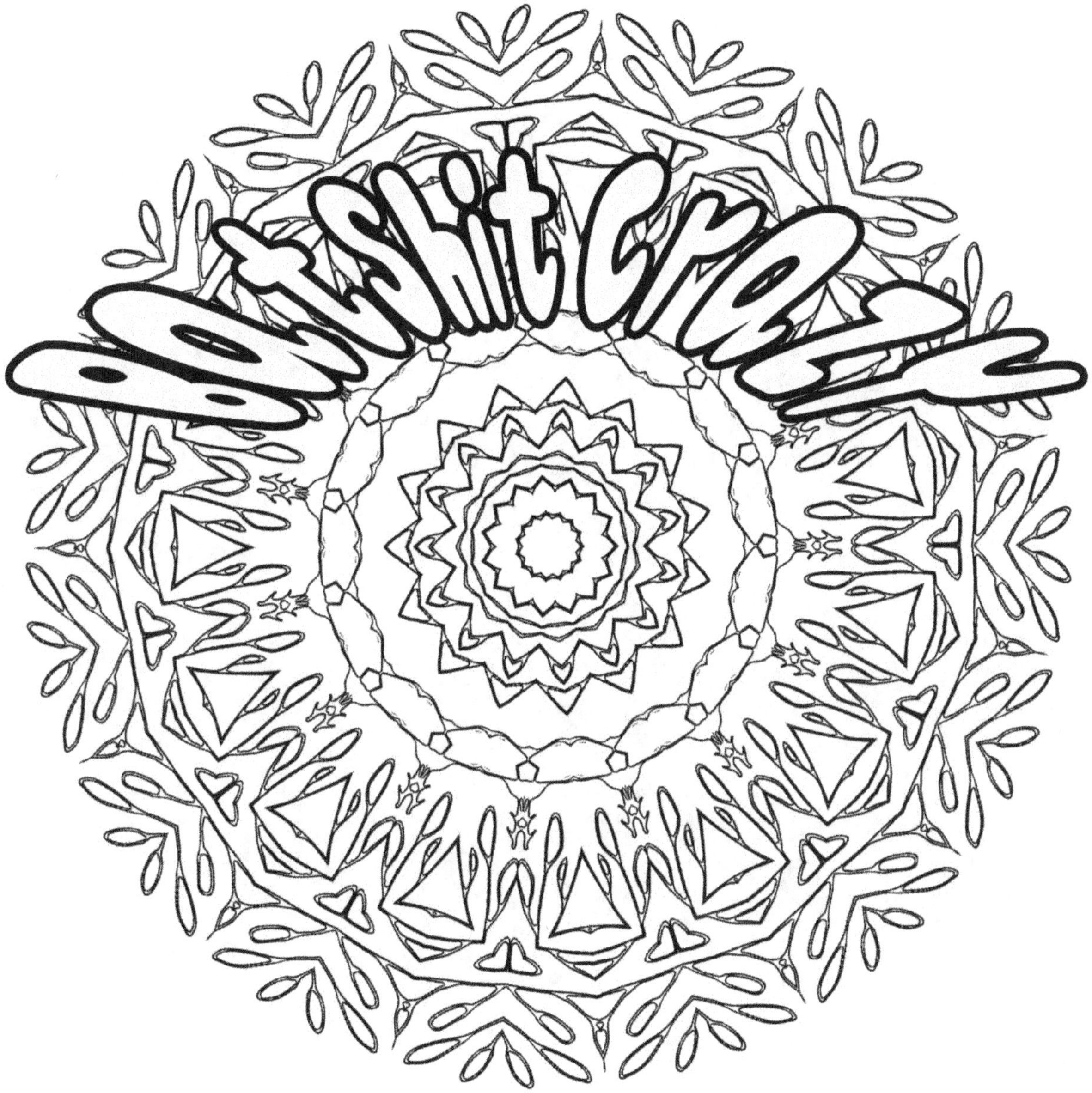
batshit crazy

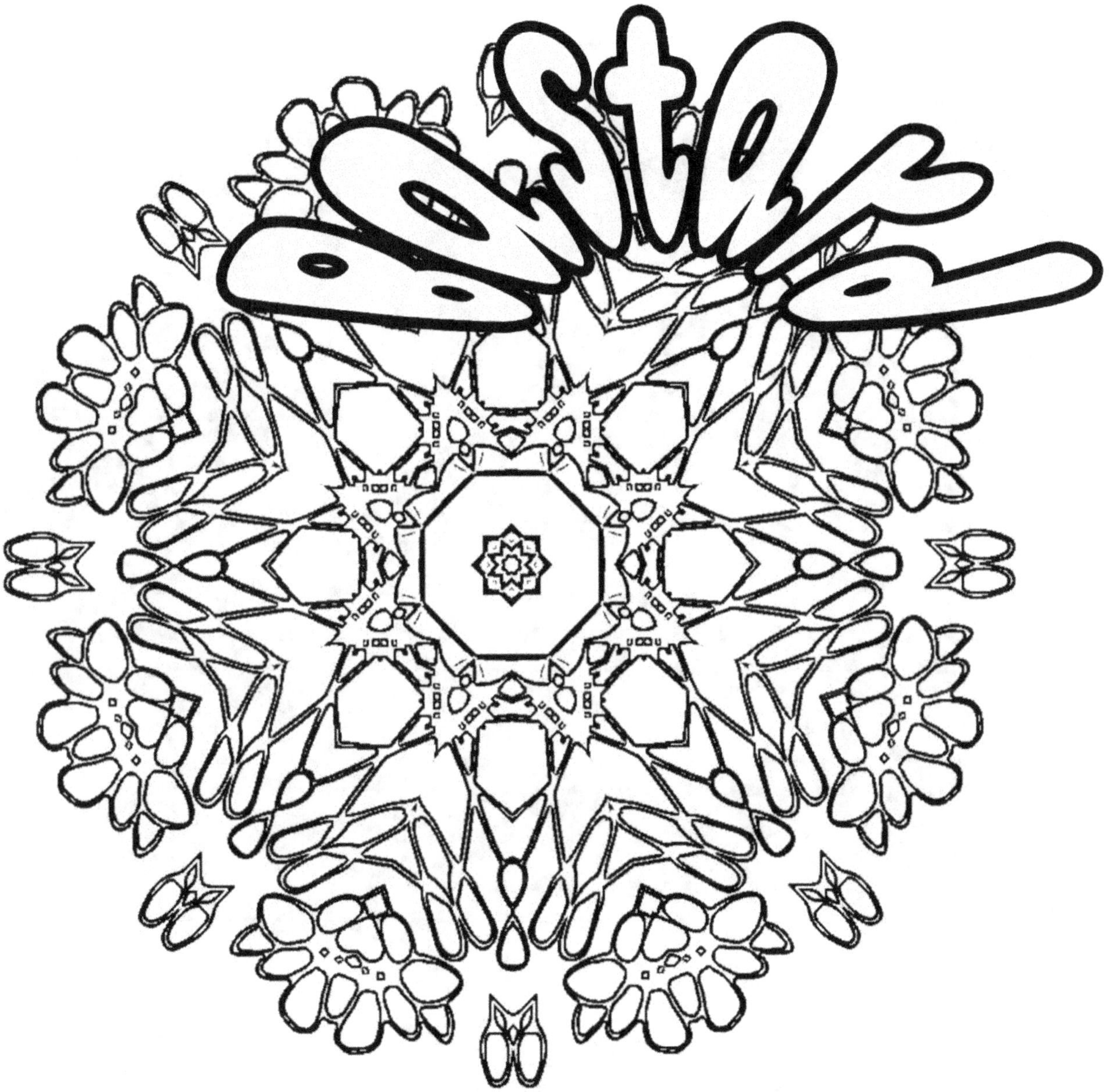
bastard

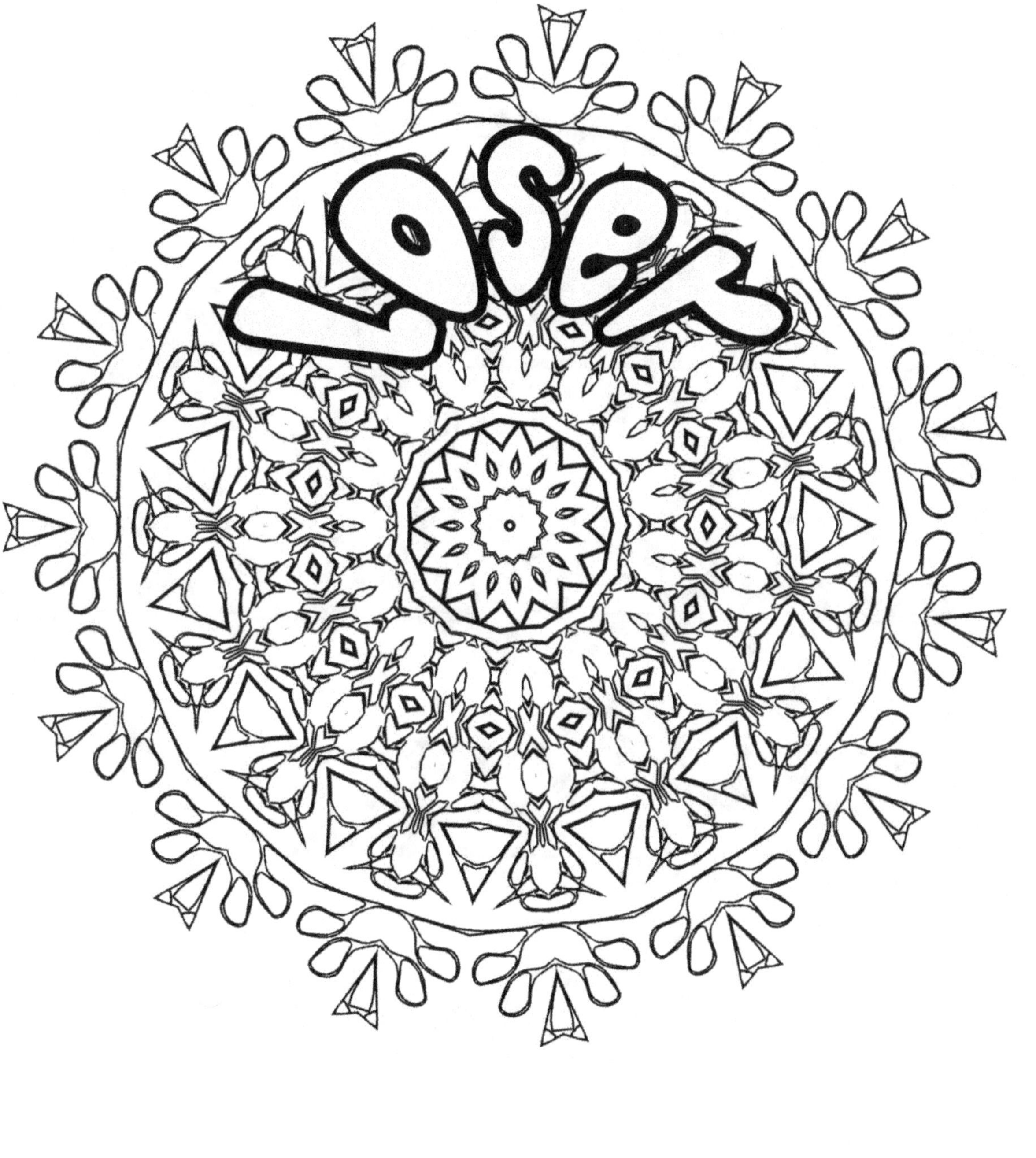
loser

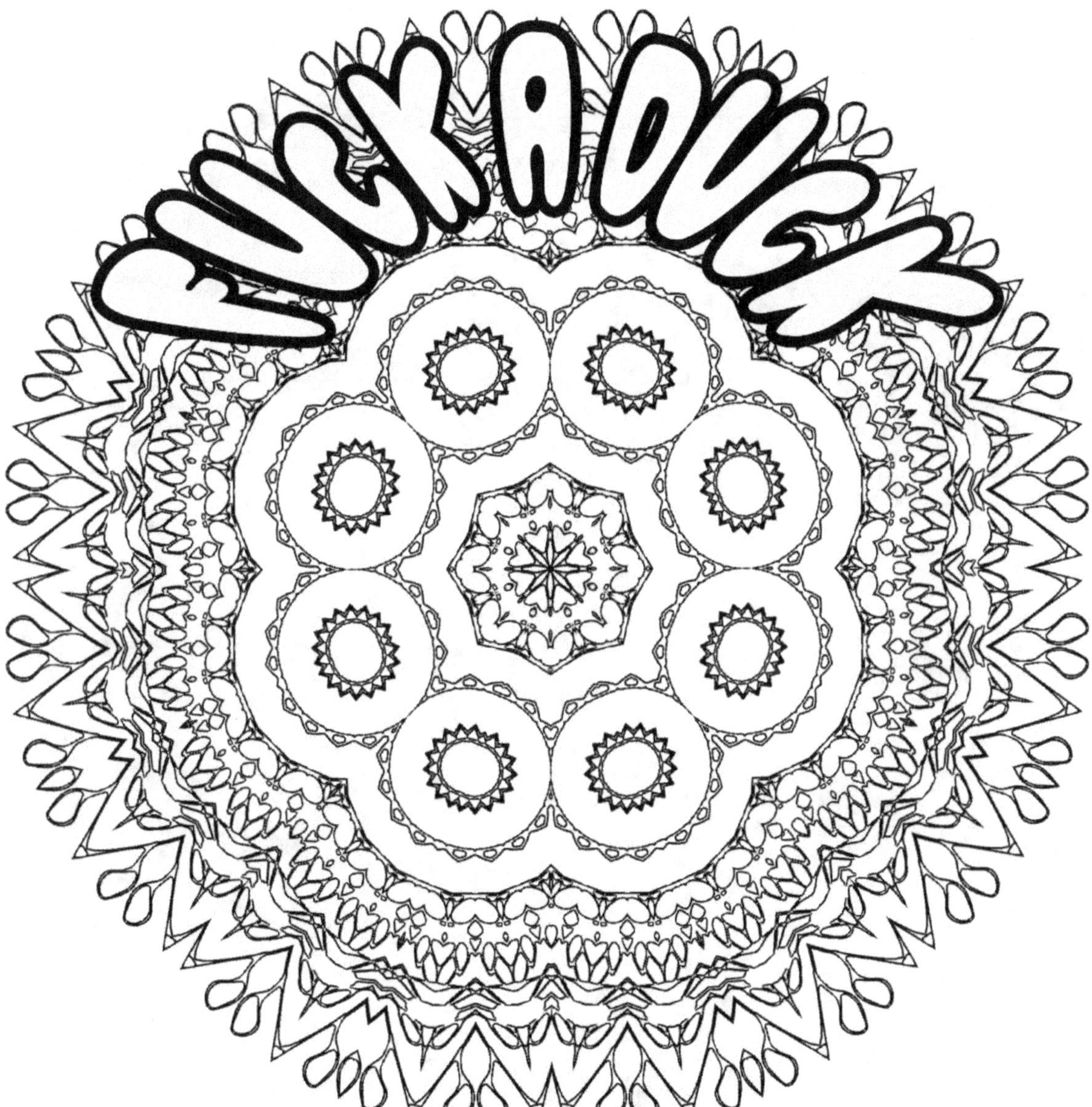
FUCK A DUCK

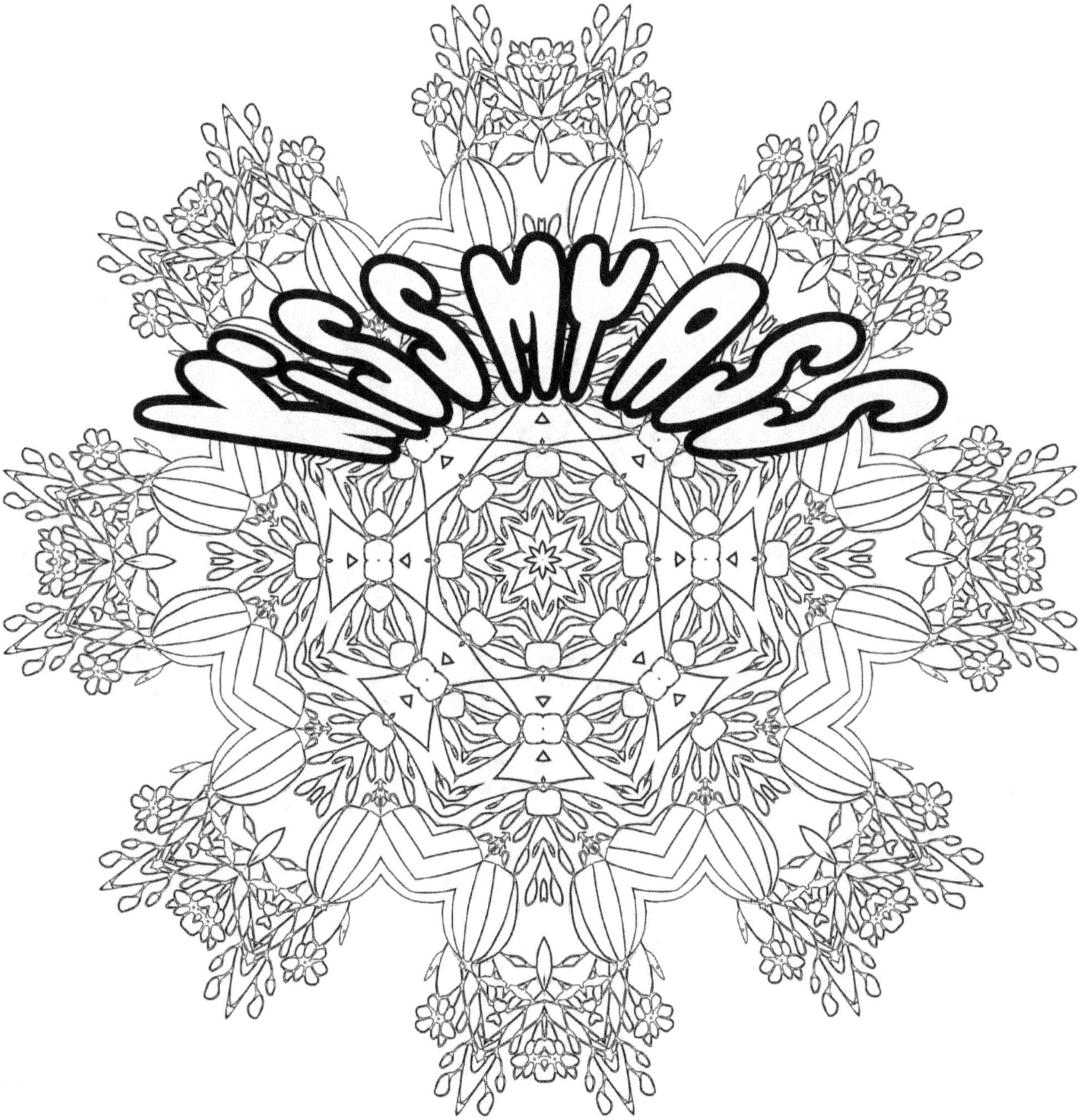
KISS MY ASS

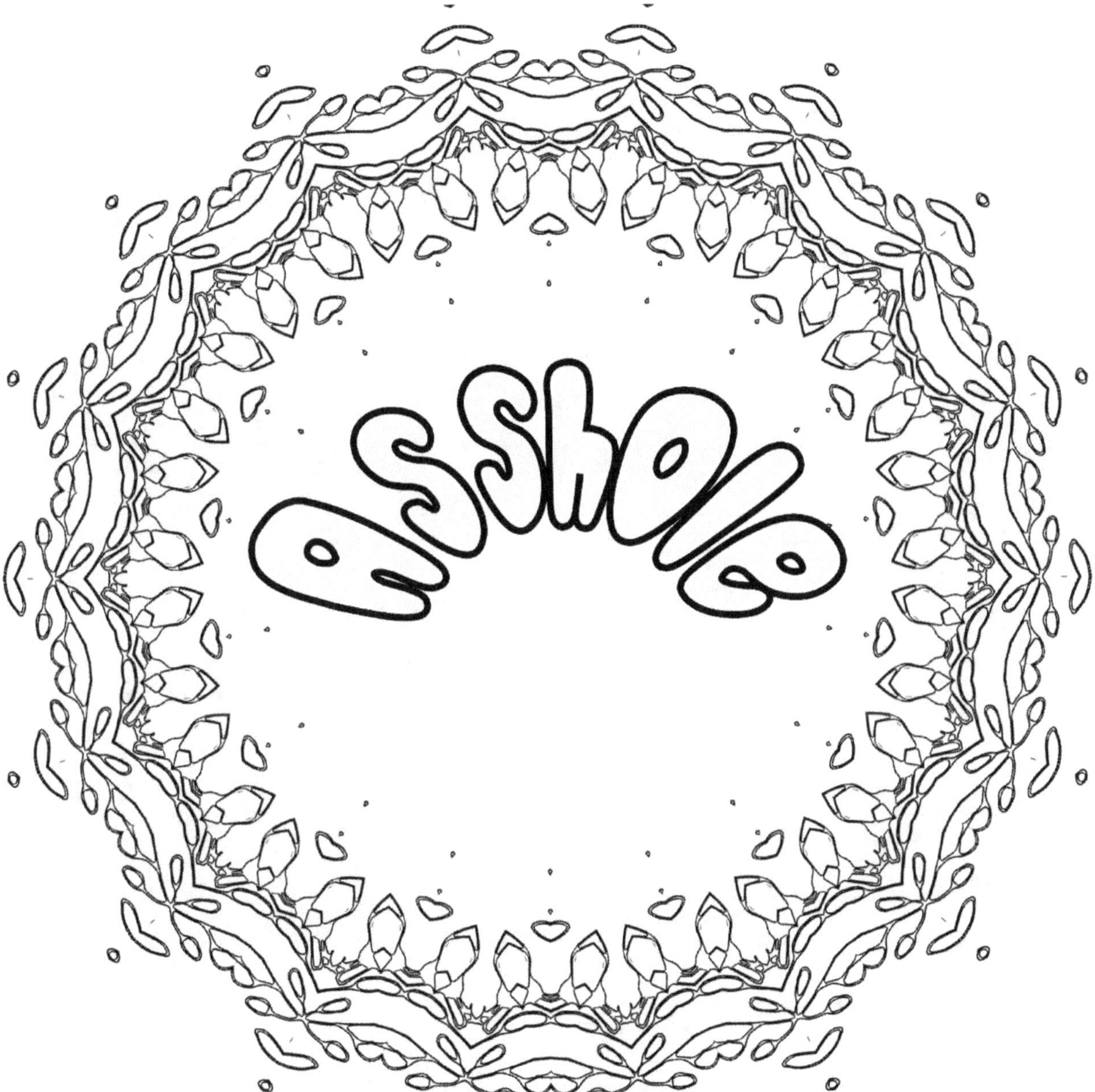
asshole

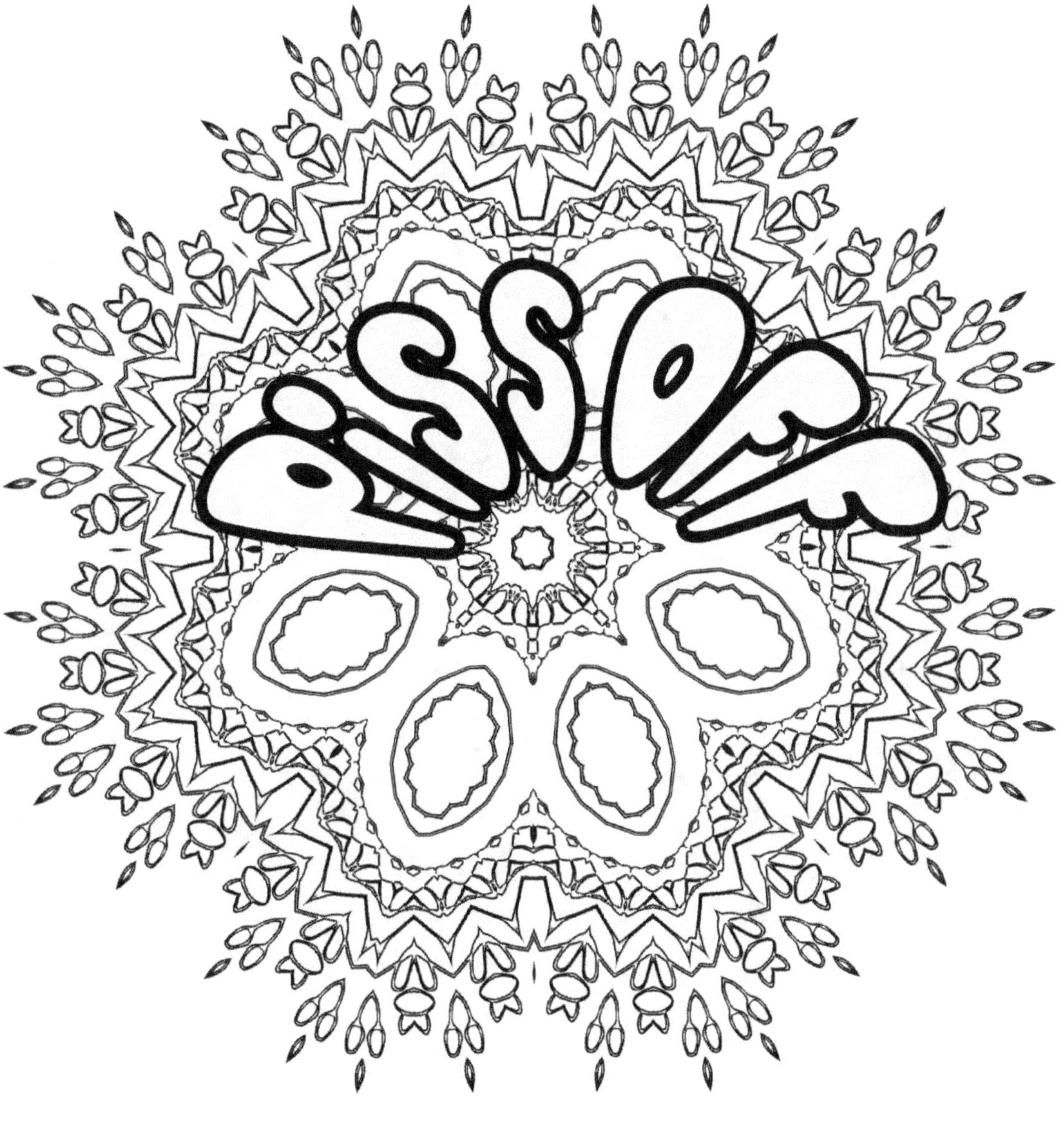
PISS OFF

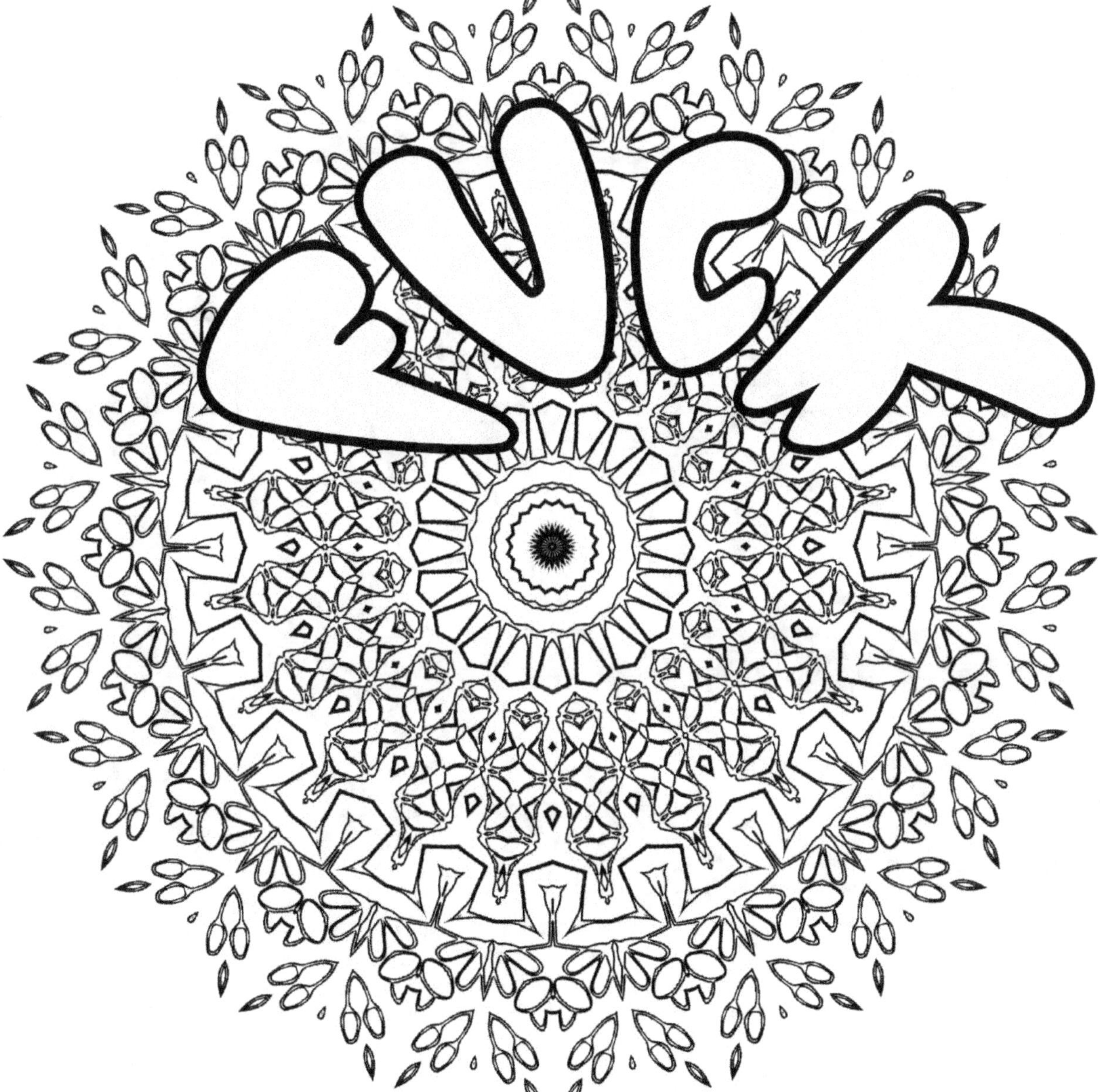
FUCK

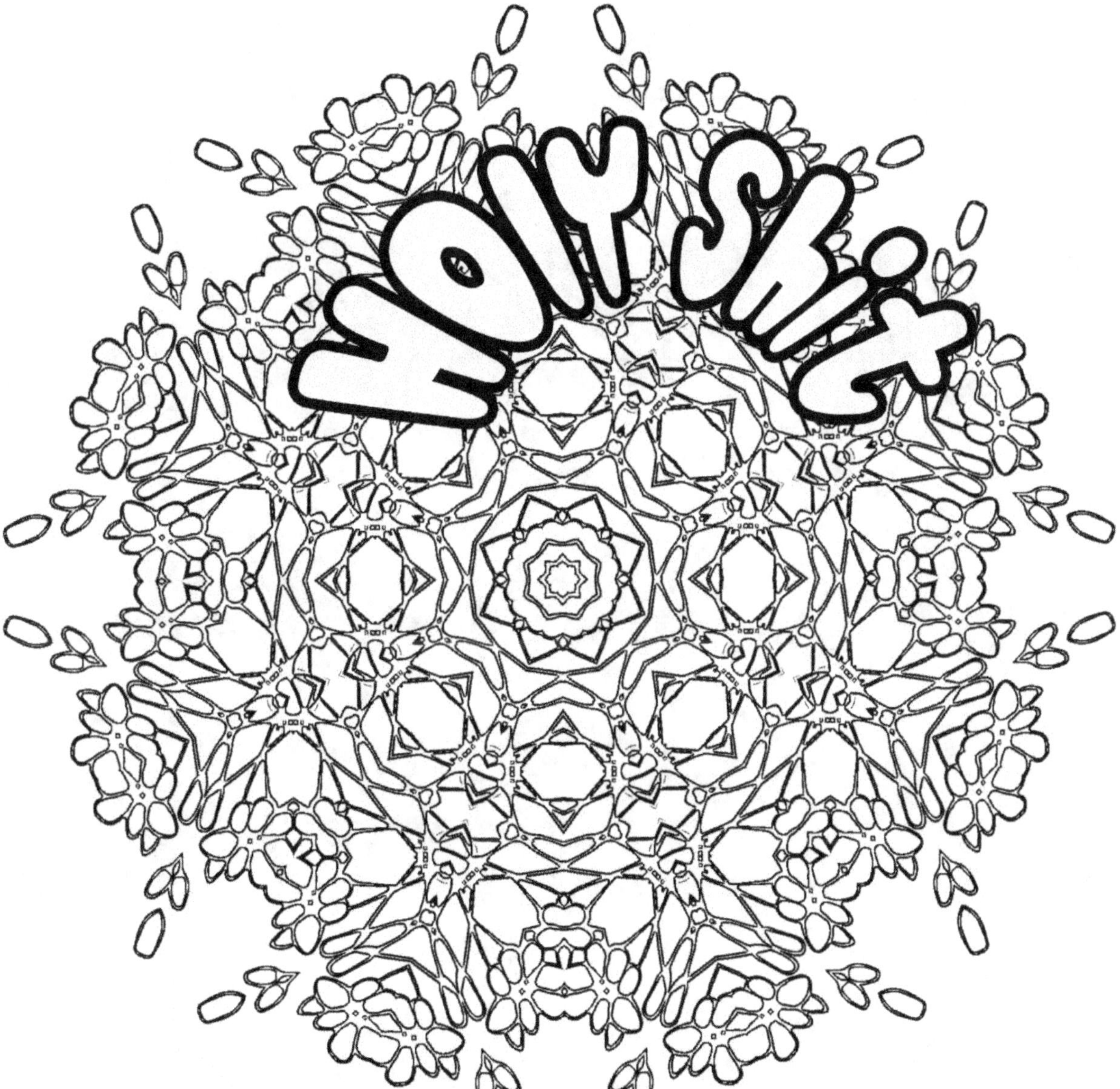
Holy Shit

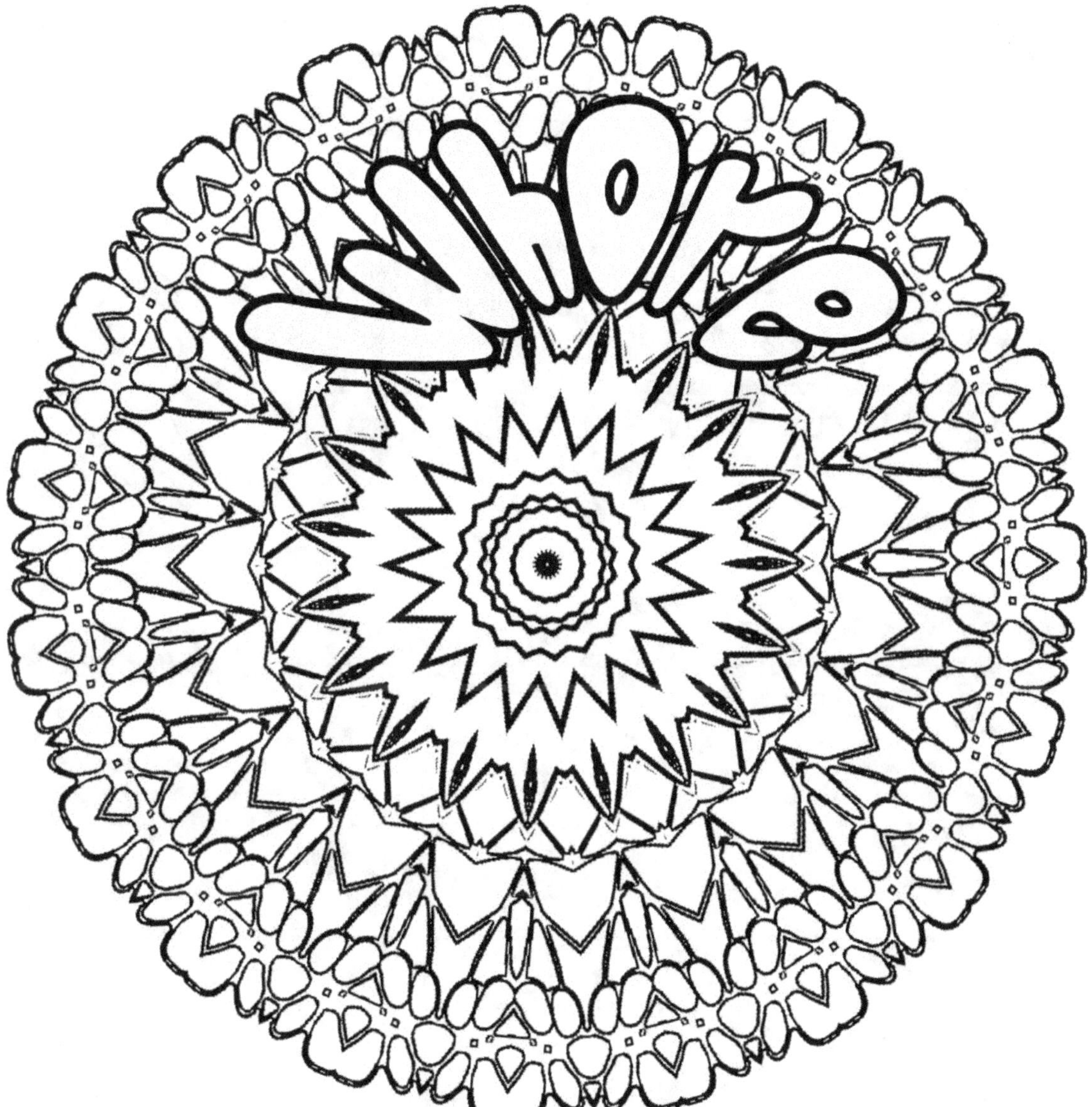
whore

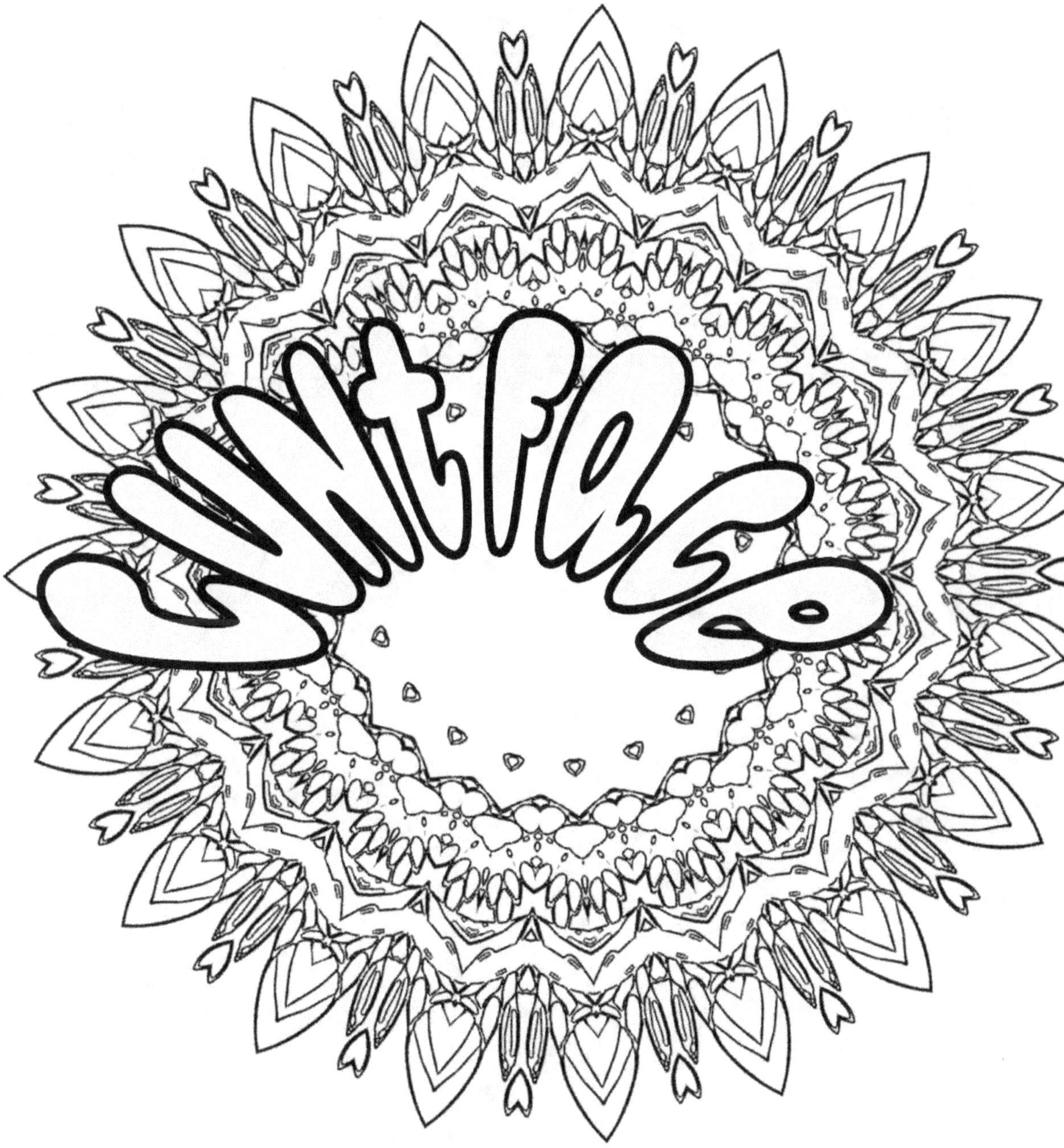
CUNT FACE

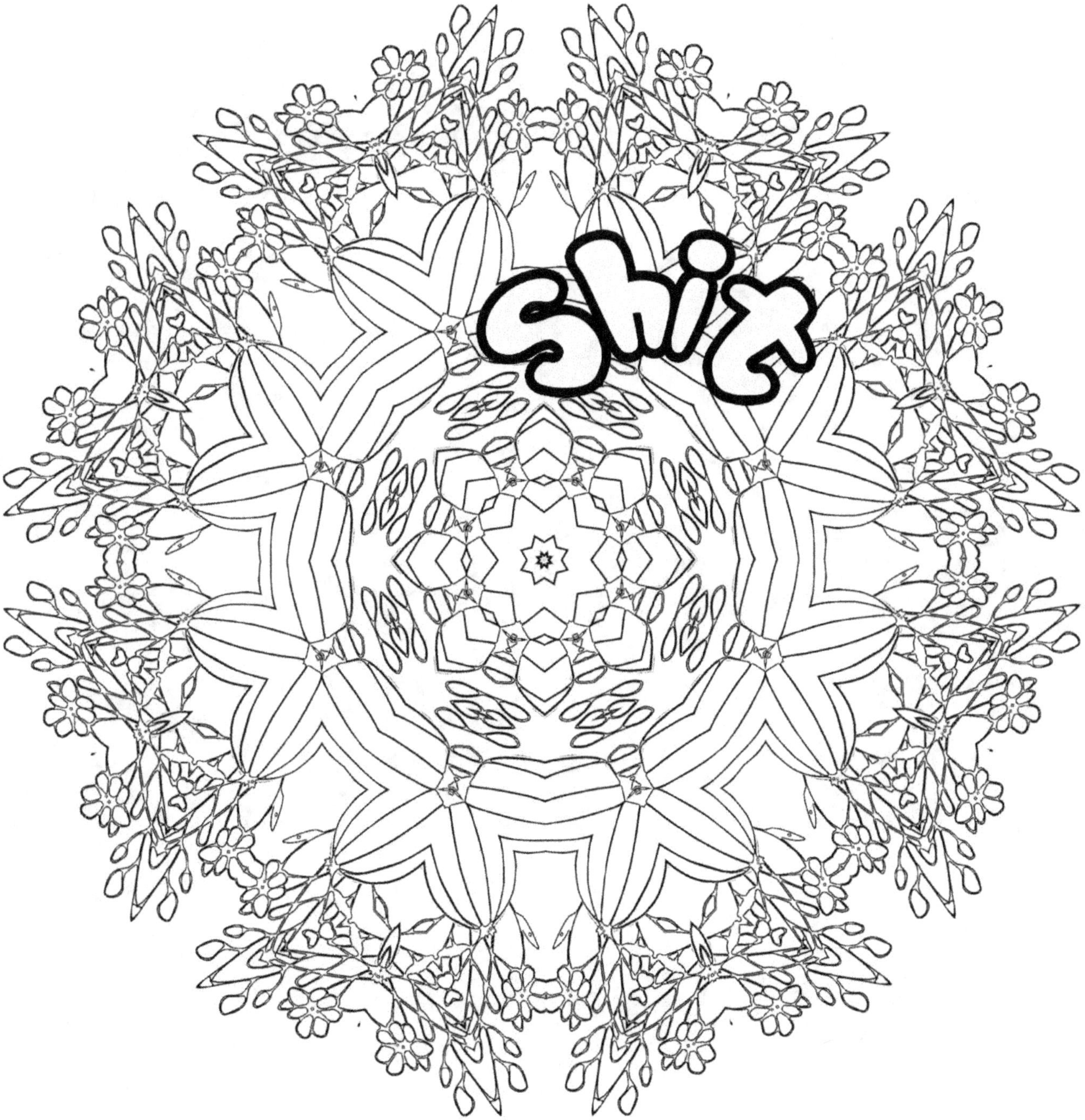
Shit

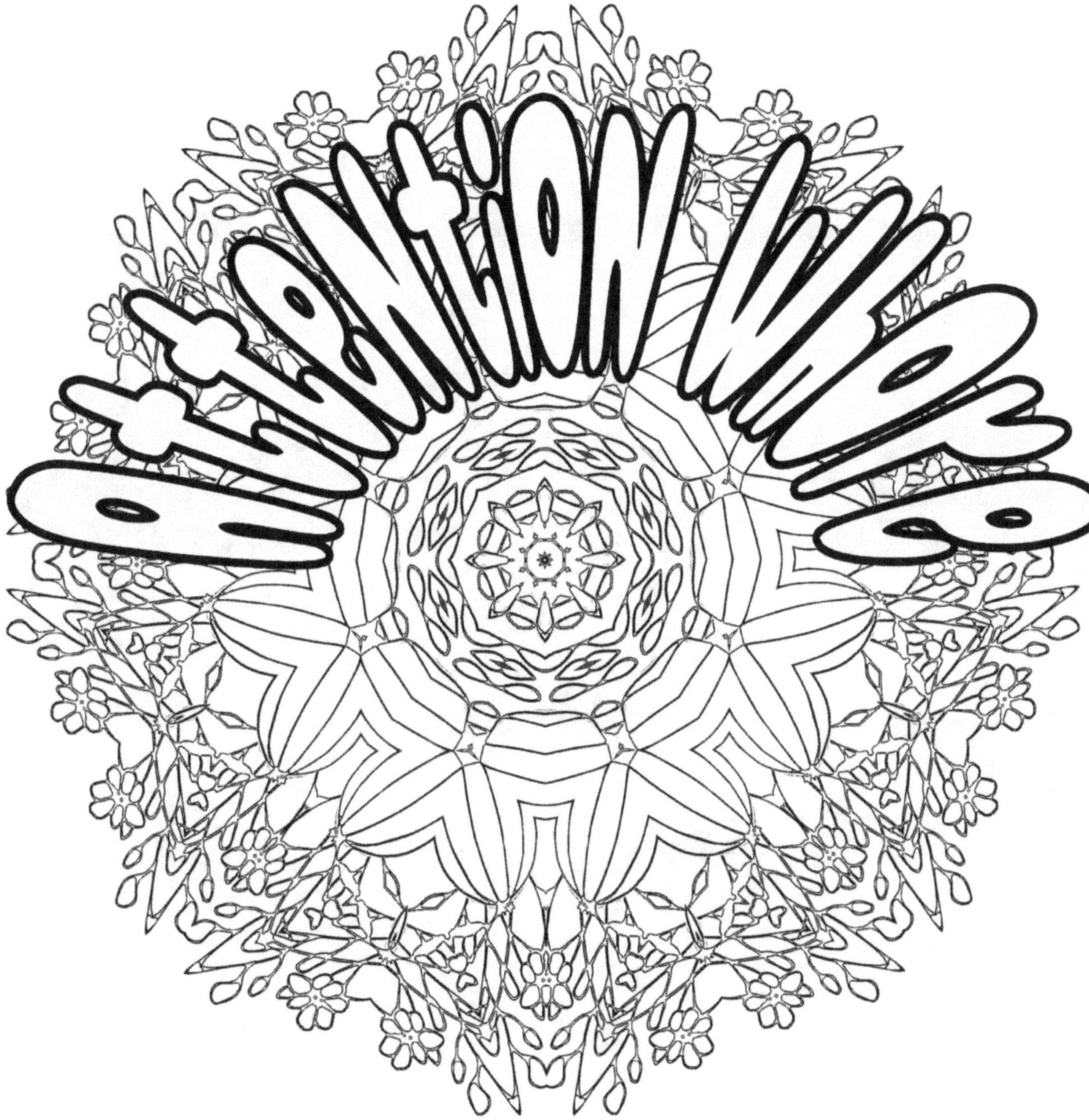
attention whore

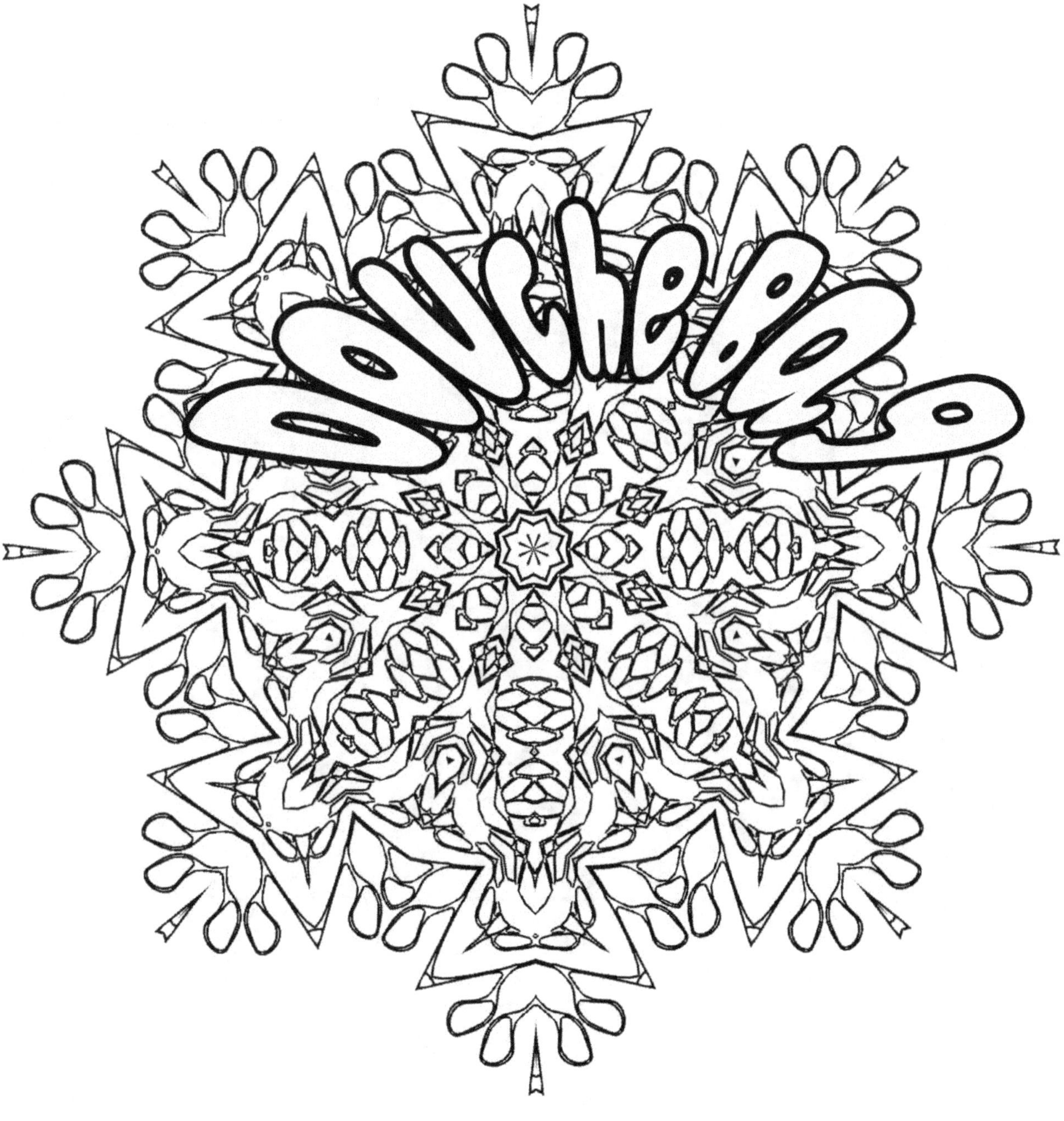
Douche Bag

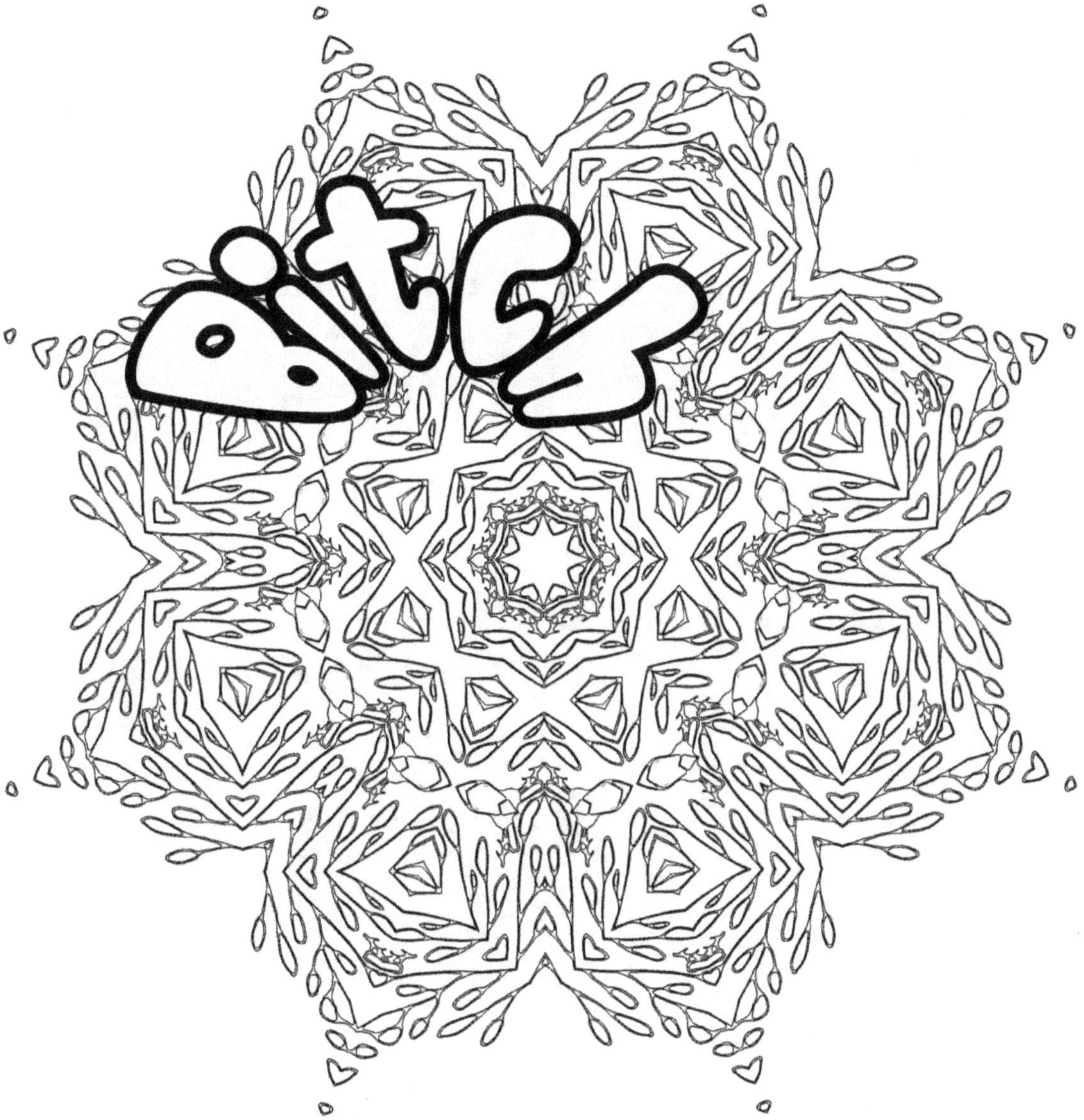
bitch

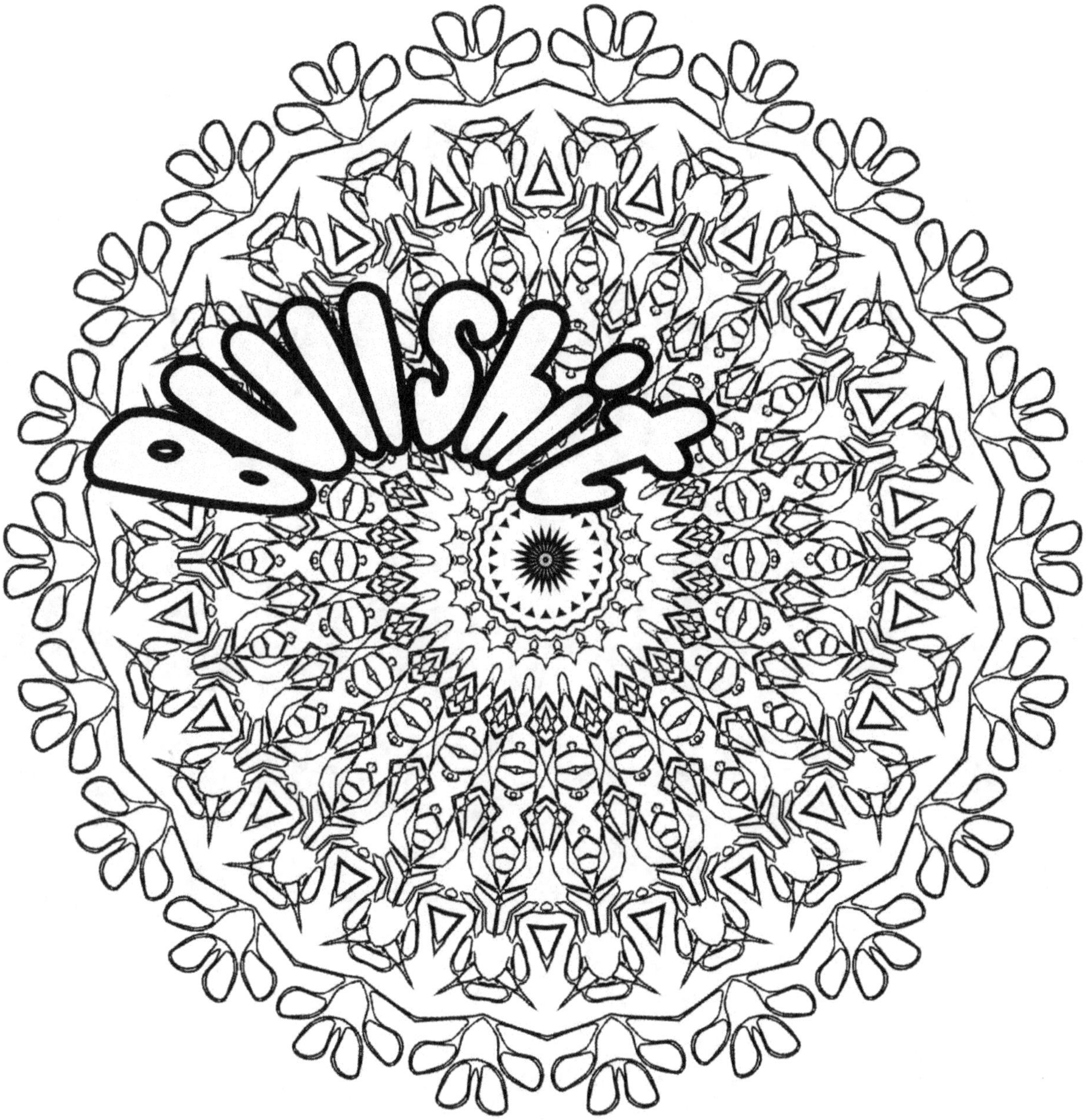
BULLSHIT

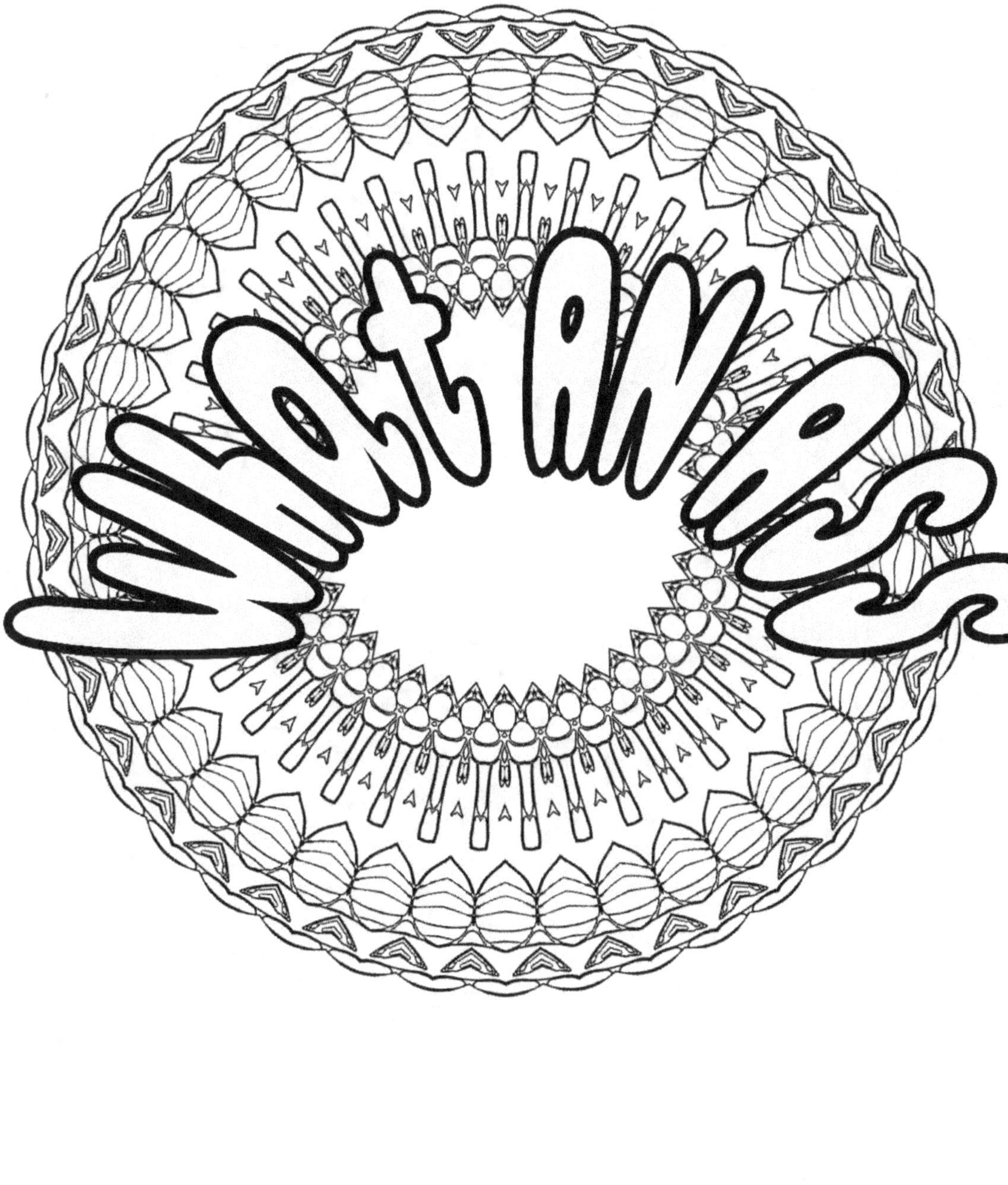
WHAT AN ASS

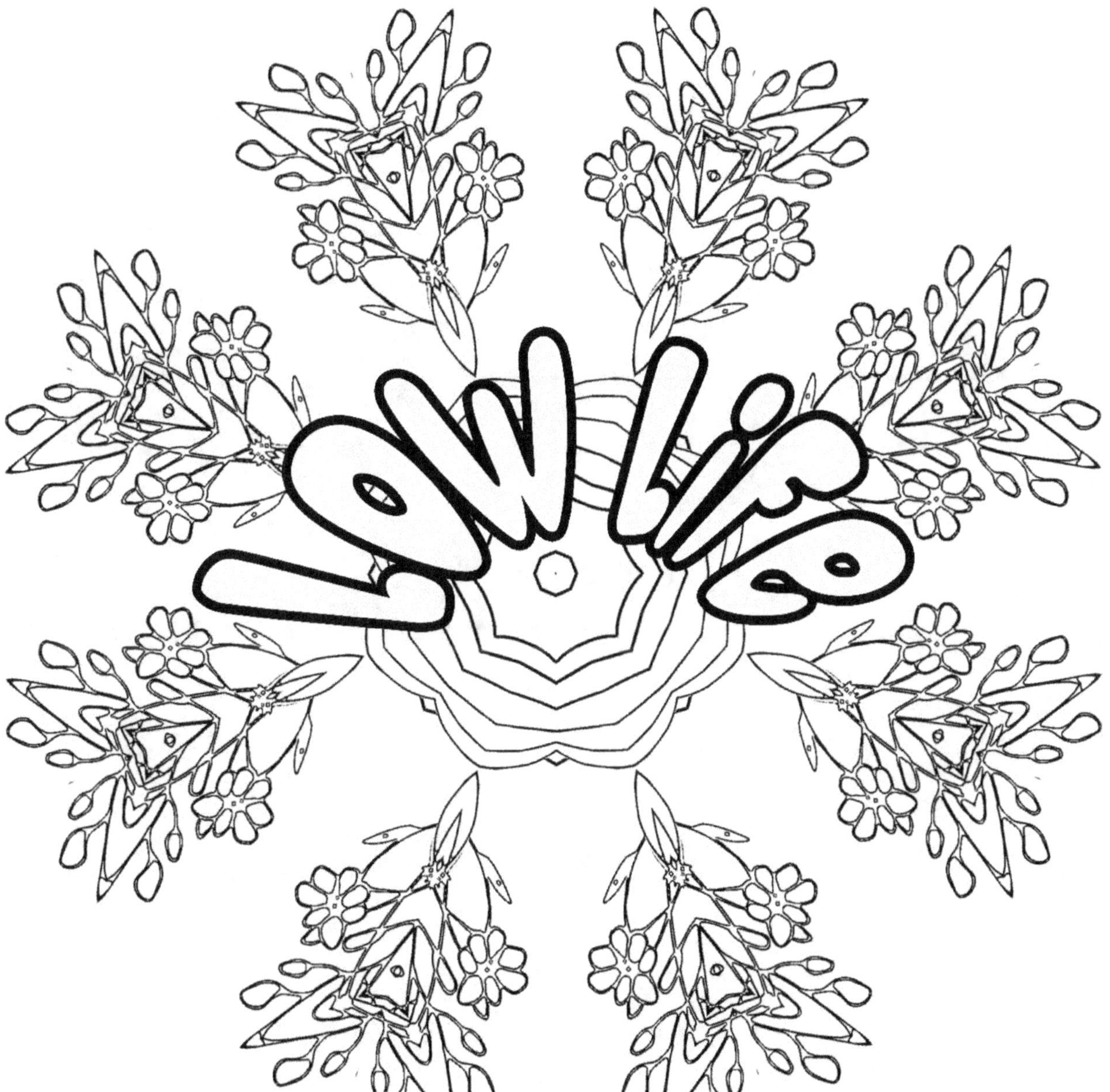
Low Life

www.ingramcontent.com/pod-product-compliance
Lightning Source LLC
Chambersburg PA
CBHW081751170526
45167CB00009B/3992
9781544115900